The Writer's Craft

Writing from Literature
Prompts from Novels and Plays

Grades 9–12

McDougal Littell Inc.
A Houghton Mifflin Company
Evanston, Illinois   Boston Dallas Phoenix

ISBN 0-8123-8907-7

7 8 9 10 – MDO – 99 98

Contents

About This Booklet

The student writing prompts in this booklet are designed to be used with twenty-two literary works frequently read by high school students. The prompts lead to types of writing taught in guided and related assignments in *The Writer's Craft* at grade levels 9, 10, 11, and 12. The chart on page iv of this booklet shows which writing modes and forms are covered for each novel or play.

Since students write best about topics in which they have a personal investment, you may wish to encourage students to explore their own responses before you provide the prompts in this booklet. Guide them in recalling thoughts and feelings sparked by their reading and by class discussions. Suggest that they look through their reading journals and learning logs for topic ideas. Then, if students need further ideas, introduce the prompts as additional thought starters. You might help students find ways to tailor the prompts to fit their own interests and ideas. Remind students who need additional support and assistance in a mode of writing suggested by a prompt that they can refer to the corresponding guided or related assignment in *The Writer's Craft* for detailed direction.

Assignment Chart

NOVELS AND PLAYS

Writing Modes and Assignments

Writing Modes and Assignments	1984	Animal Farm	Great Expectations	The Grapes of Wrath	The Great Gatsby	Huckleberry Finn	Lord of the Flies	Of Mice and Men	The Red Badge of Courage	The Scarlet Letter	A Separate Peace
Personal and Expressive Writing	•	•	•	•	•	•	•	•	•	•	•
Observation and Description	•	•	•	•	•	•			•	•	
Narrative and Literary Writing	•								•		
Informative Exposition: Classification	•	•	•	•	•		•	•	•		•
Informative Exposition: Analysis	•					•	•				•
Informative Exposition: Synthesis	•	•							•	•	
Persuasion	•	•	•	•	•	•	•	•	•	•	
Responding to Literature	•	•	•	•	•	•	•	•	•	•	

NOVELS AND PLAYS

Writing Modes and Assignments

Writing Modes and Assignments	A Tale of Two Cities	To Kill a Mockingbird	Wuthering Heights	The Crucible	Death of a Salesman	The Glass Menagerie	Julius Caesar	Macbeth	Our Town	Romeo and Juliet	The Odyssey
Personal and Expressive Writing	•	•	•	•	•		•		•	•	•
Observation and Description	•	•					•	•		•	
Narrative and Literary Writing	•		•	•		•			•		•
Informative Exposition: Classification	•	•	•			•	•		•		
Informative Exposition: Analysis		•	•		•						•
Informative Exposition: Synthesis	•			•	•	•	•	•	•		
Persuasion	•	•	•			•	•	•	•	•	•
Responding to Literature	•	•	•	•		•	•		•	•	•

1984
by George Orwell

1. Personal and Expressive Writing

- **Personal Letter** George Orwell died in 1950. Imagine that he is still alive, and write him a letter sharing some of your responses to *1984*. In what ways do you feel that his warnings are still relevant, although almost fifty years have passed since he wrote the novel? Do you feel more or less hopeful about the future than Orwell seems to have felt?

2. Observation and Description

- **Eyewitness Report** Think about the world Orwell describes in *1984*. Are we moving toward that world? Report on an episode you witnessed that you feel reflects a move toward the conditions depicted in *1984*. Record sensory details, dialogue, and action so that your readers feel they are witnessing the event.

3. Narrative and Literary Writing

- **Story** Remember the Parsons' seven-year-old girl, the avid member of the Spies who turns her father in to be tortured? Write an episode that could be part of a story about her life twenty years later. Give the girl a name, and have her recall the events of her childhood. Think about how the London of *1984* might change in twenty years, about the kind of adult the girl might become, about her relationship to the Party, and about the conflicts she might experience. Choose details that will bring the setting, characters, and plot of your story to life for your readers.

4. Informative Exposition: Classification

- **Explaining Concepts and Ideas** You've just been hired by the Ministry of Truth. Your first job is to write a speech explaining the dangers of learning about the past. You have been instructed to use that disgusting old derelict, Winston Smith, as an example of what happens to someone who does not heed such dangers. You may write your speech in standard English, or you may try your hand at Newspeak.

5. Informative Exposition: Analysis

• **Examining Changes** "Oranges and lemons, say the bells of St. Clements. . . ." Winston finds special meaning in the familiar children's song. By the end of the novel, however, the Thought Police have given the old song a chilling new significance. In an essay of analysis, explore what the song originally seems to mean to Winston. Then show how its meaning changes—for Winston and for you—over the course of the novel.

6. Informative Exposition: Synthesis

• **Extended Response** George Orwell's *1984* depicts what was, to him, a distant, imaginary future. Learn what the real world was like in 1984. Find out about living conditions as well as governments and political events in major countries of the West and the Third World. Then, in an essay, show how one or more ideas from Orwell's novel did or did not "come true." Refer to details from the novel, as well as to facts about specific countries and events of the real year 1984, as you explain your findings. Be sure to credit your sources correctly.

7. Persuasion

• **Persuasive Essay** Hold on—thanks to complex new technology, you're about to be transported to the London of *1984*. You will stay just long enough to distribute a pamphlet urging people to take action against the government of Big Brother, and then you will be whisked safely home. Write what your pamphlet will say. First, decide whether to target the proles, the Outer Party members, or the Inner Party members as your principal audience. Which persuasive techniques will most effectively rouse them? In planning the actions you will suggest, ask yourself what strengths the members of your audience have, and what strategies would work best against Big Brother and the Thought Police.

8. Responding to Literature

• **Personal Response** Three major forces in *1984* are hate, love, and fear. Which of the three do you think Orwell considered strongest? Which do you consider strongest? In a personal response essay, use specific details from *1984* and from your own experience to explain and support your answers.

Copyright © McDougal, Littell & Company

Animal Farm
by George Orwell

1. Personal and Expressive Writing

- **Journal Writing to Public Writing** Mr. Jones finally pushes the animals too far. Write a series of entries in your journal about a time when you felt pushed too far—or when you pushed someone else too far. Reflect on what happened, on why it happened, and on how you felt. Then focus on one of your journal writings and develop it into a piece of public writing.

2. Observation and Description

- **Focused Description** The time: the year 2000. The place: Animal Farm. The scene: what do you imagine? Write a focused description of the future that you foresee for Animal Farm. Take into account the changes the pigs and other animals have undergone by the end of the novel. Then describe the farm as you imagine it might be in the future, including a brief summary of the events that have occurred between the end of the novel and the year 2000.

3. Informative Exposition: Classification

- **Comparison and Contrast** Napoleon and Snowball—what a pair. In an essay, compare and contrast these two characters, mentioning strengths as well as weaknesses of each. Use details and examples from the novel, and end your comparison by explaining which of this pair of porkers you consider better suited to be leader.

4. Informative Exposition: Synthesis

- **Extended Response** *Animal Farm* can be read as a satire of the history of the former U.S.S.R. From an encyclopedia or a historical reference work, learn about Russia's October Revolution of 1917 and the events that followed. Continue researching the period up to Stalin's pact with Hitler in 1939. Then write an essay showing how one or more of the events you have learned about is reflected in *Animal Farm.* Be sure to credit your sources correctly as you write your essay.

5. Persuasion

- **Supporting Opinions** Mr. Jones's use of violence outrages the animals—yet they use violence themselves to drive away the humans. Do you think that violence can be justified if it is used for a good cause? Or do you think that violence is never acceptable? Explain your opinion in a persuasive essay, using details from the novel and from your experience to support your points.

- **Satire** *Animal Farm* may be viewed as a satirical fable that criticizes several aspects of government. Write a satirical spinoff from *Animal Farm,* focusing on a current situation of concern to you. For your fable, make it clear how your setting or characters are linked to those of *Animal Farm.* Then use exaggeration or humor to call attention to a modern problem and show that change is needed.

6. Responding to Literature

- **Personal Response** What effect does being in a position of power have upon people? Does having power over others change people for the better or for the worse? In an essay, discuss your views and show how the characters in *Animal Farm* support your position.

Great Expectations
by Charles Dickens

1. Personal and Expressive Writing

- **Autobiographical Incident** Pip's life is shaped, for better or for worse, by help from others—and by his own willingness to help. Write about a time in your childhood when you received or gave some important help. Show what happened, who was involved, how you felt about the event at the time, and why you now consider it important.

2. Observation and Description

- **Character Sketch** Who can forget Pumblechook, Miss Havisham, Wemmick and his Aged P., or Abel Magwitch? Dickens is famous for his characters. Review the novel and study Dickens's way of creating characters. Use what you learn to create your own Dickensian character and write a character sketch for that character. Give your character a name and include details that reveal the personality of your character to your readers.

3. Narrative and Literary Writing

- **Short Story** Get set—you're about to board the Dickens-o-Matic time machine! You'll be whisked back to spend an hour with Pip and his friends at any point in Pip's life. While you're there, you'll be allowed to give one gift to one person. Your gift may be a physical object or it may be a piece of information. Write the story of your trip and its consequences. Tell where you land, who and what you see, what you do, and the outcome of your adventure.

4. Informative Exposition: Classification

- **Comparison and Contrast** Does being wealthy assure happiness? Compare and contrast two characters in the novel, one from the working class and one who is wealthy. Who is happier? What do you think Dickens is saying about the relationship between wealth and happiness? Do you agree or disagree?

5. Persuasion

- **Persuasive Essay** *Great Expectations* appeared as a magazine serial before it was published as a novel. The serialized version ends with no hope of a further relationship between Pip and Estella. However, when the novel was published, Dickens bowed to public pressure and changed the ending. Write a persuasive letter to Dickens, explaining why you think he should or shouldn't have changed the ending. Think about whether you feel the present ending fits the novel's characters and themes.

- **Debate** "Magwitch's money does Pip more harm than good." Write a four-minute opening speech for the affirmative or negative team in a debate of this proposition. Support your points with details about the advantages or disadvantages that Pip's "great expectations" bring him. Deal with opposing arguments and make your reasoning clear. As a challenge, you may wish to write two openings, one for the affirmative and one for the negative.

6. Responding to Literature

- **Literary Analysis** Imagine that you are Miss Havisham writing your autobiography. Write either a section entitled "What I Would Do Differently" or "Lessons I've Learned." Think about Miss Havisham's goals, actions, and her relationships with Pip and with Estella.

- **Personal Response** What does the title of the novel mean to you? In an essay, explain what the expectations are and who has these expectations. Reflect on what you learned from the novel about the expectations one might have during youth.

The Grapes of Wrath
by John Steinbeck

1. Personal and Expressive Writing

- **Autobiographical Incident** The Joads live with injustice and loss. Write about an incident in which you experienced the unfair loss of something you valued. You may focus on a tangible loss, such as the theft of an item you owned, or an intangible loss, such as losing a competition, losing a sense of confidence, or losing a friendship. Show what you lost, what it meant to you, how you felt and responded, and how the event has affected you since.

2. Observation and Description

- **Oral History** No one who lived through the Great Depression will ever forget it, and few emerged from it unchanged. Interview someone who recalls the period. Find out where your subject was living, how your subject's family made ends meet, and how your subject feels that the depression has influenced him or her. Write your interview as an oral history, pointing out likenesses and differences in your subject's experiences and the experiences of the characters in *The Grapes of Wrath.*

3. Informative Exposition: Classification

- **Comparison and Contrast** Steinbeck's Dust Bowl migrants in their tarpaulin-covered pickup trucks are, in some ways, not so different from the pioneers of an earlier century in their covered wagons. Yet in other ways, the two groups are very different indeed. If you had to join one group or the other, which would you choose, and why? Explain your answer in an essay comparing and contrasting the Dust Bowl migrants and the earlier pioneers. Consider what each group was leaving and traveling toward, what hardships each group experienced along the way, and what resources each group could draw upon.

4. Informative Exposition: Synthesis

- **Extended Response** As *The Grapes of Wrath* shows, efforts to form workers' unions were born of desperation, and those efforts met with fear, suspicion, and violence. Find out more about the labor union movement of the 1920s and 30s and about the conditions that gave rise to it. For example, you might learn about and focus on one or two of the following: the economic policies of President Herbert Hoover (after whom the "Hoovervilles" were named), about FDR's New Deal, about why the epithet "Red" was so inflammatory, and about union-busting practices such as blacklisting and planting "stools" (stool pigeons). Then write an essay using what you have learned to explain more fully one or more events in the novel. Be sure to credit your sources correctly.

5. Persuasion

- **Argument Analysis** The year is 1939, and you can't believe your good luck. You've just landed a job as a reporter for the monthly magazine *Our Bakersfield.* You hope to defuse local tensions, and maybe make a name for yourself, by writing an article about the conflict between the migrant workers and the growers. In your article, show both groups' positions, pointing out that both sides have reasonable and understandable concerns. Use details from *The Grapes of Wrath,* but try to present an unbiased view of the conflict.

6. Responding to Literature

- **Interpretive Essay** Why do you think Steinbeck calls his novel *The Grapes of Wrath?* Examine the first verse of Julia Ward Howe's song "The Battle Hymn of the Republic," from which Steinbeck took his title. (You might also look up the Book of Isaiah, chapter 63, verse 3, in the Bible; these lines are cited as Julia Ward Howe's inspiration.) Then, in an essay, explain what you think the "grapes of wrath" are, what causes the wrath, and what the Joads and their friends have to do with these "grapes of wrath." Support your interpretation with quotations from the novel.

The Great Gatsby
by F. Scott Fitzgerald

1. Personal and Expressive Writing

- **Personal Letter** Well-defined characters in a story can seem as real as people we actually know. Write a letter to a friend and describe Nick as if he were an acquaintance or a friend of yours. Include details about his character and personality as well as a description of his physical characteristics. To help you decide what kind of person Nick is and what you might say about him, skim the novel again noticing Nick's actions toward Jordan, Daisy, Tom, and Gatsby.

2. Observation and Description

- **Observing Situations and Settings** Often, it doesn't take much to bring to mind the details of people and places that have made a strong impression. Whenever Nick thinks of Long Island, he thinks of Jay Gatsby. Think of a place that you associate with a particular person. You might wish to freewrite about the person and place to gather rich sensory details. Then choose specific details that describe the person and the place and show what each means to you.

3. Informative Exposition: Classification

- **Using Comparison and Contrast** How does the phrase "appearances can be deceiving" relate to the situations and characters portrayed in *The Great Gatsby?* In an essay, compare outward appearances as presented in the novel to the reality behind the appearances.

- **Definition** In the United States, one of the benefits of equality is the possibility that anyone may set and achieve high goals and material success. This ideal is sometimes referred to as the American dream. How would you define the American dream? What do you see as the goals most people set? How are the goals and desires of people today like or unlike those of the characters in *The Great Gatsby?*

4. Informative Exposition: Synthesis

- **Advice Essay** Imagine that you are an old school friend of Daisy's. Just after Nick has reintroduced her to Gatsby, she asks you for advice. In an essay, sum up what you see as her biggest problem. Is it the need to choose between Gatsby and Tom? Or is it something deeper? Then tell her what you think she should do, and show her how your solution will benefit her.

5. Persuasion

- **Argument Analysis** Gatsby might be viewed as a phony and a swindler. Yet Nick sees him as a person of integrity: "Gatsby turned out all right at the end," Nick maintains (and to Gatsby he says, "You're worth the whole damn bunch put together"). In an essay, show how both of these opposing views of Gatsby are true. Refer to details from the novel to explain and support both views.

- **Persuasive Essay** If you could make a wish and suddenly be part of one of the social groups in the novel, which one would you choose? Would you want to be part of Tom and Daisy's wealthy crowd, Gatsby's wild and newly rich group, Nick's business group who are still trying to make their fortunes, or working class people like Myrtle and her husband? In a persuasive essay, explain which group you would rather be part of and why belonging to that group would be best.

6. Responding to Literature

- **Personal Response** In the first and last chapters of *The Great Gatsby,* Nick, the narrator, stresses the importance of dreams. What do you think F. Scott Fitzgerald is saying about the place of dreams in peoples' lives? In an essay, state one idea about dreams that you think he is expressing, and show how he expresses it. Explain how your own feelings about dreams fit in, or don't fit in, with Fitzgerald's.

- **Critical Analysis** Were there aspects of the plot, characters, or setting that were particularly meaningful to you? Were there elements that were especially troubling or that didn't ring true? Choose some aspect of the novel and in a critical analysis show why that aspect of the novel did or did not work well for you as a reader.

Huckleberry Finn
by Mark Twain

1. Personal and Expressive Writing

- **Memoir** Like Huck's days drifting on the river, some memories evoke a sense of freedom and peace. Write a memoir about a time when you felt peaceful and free. Choose a specific event as your focus, and include vivid details to show the place, the time, the people, and the meaning the event had for you.

2. Observation and Description

- **Character Sketch** Huck's description of "Pap" reveals the distrust and fear that the man inspires in Huck; his descriptions of Jim and Tom reveal the warmth Huck feels for his two friends. In a character sketch, describe someone you know well. Portray your subject in action, and choose details that show your subject's looks and personality, as well as your feelings for him or her.

3. Narrative and Literary Writing

- **Dramatic Scene** Write one or more dramatic scenes showing what becomes of Huck after he "lights out for the territory" at the end of *Huckleberry Finn.* You might portray Huck as an older teenager, a young adult, or a mature man. What new experiences has he had? How has he changed since his boyhood, and how has he remained the same? Is he still in touch with Jim and Tom? What does he find most satisfying about his present life, and what conflicts does he feel? What plans or ambitions does he have?

4. Informative Exposition: Analysis

- **Examining Changes** Imagine that you're Tom Sawyer. You knew Huck before he took off on his raft, and you've spent time with him again at the end of his trip. Write an essay of analysis, examining the changes you see in Huck. How is he different now from the old Huck who didn't (much) mind Miss Watson's attempts at "sivilizin'" him? How is he the same? Do you think he has become more or less civilized? Frame your essay as a letter home to one of the former members of Tom Sawyer's Gang.

5. Informative Exposition: Synthesis

- **Drawing Conclusions** Think about the experiences Huck had and the people he met in the summer recounted in the novel. What conclusions about human nature—about how people behave—can you draw from these experiences? Choose one episode and show what it demonstrates about human nature. Present your conclusions in an informative essay. Be sure to use details from the novel as evidence to support your conclusions.

6. Persuasion

- **Editorial** As the editor of the *Mississippi Gazette,* you distribute your newspaper to many of the small towns along the river south of Cairo. Write an editorial expressing your views about the tarring and feathering of "the king" and "the duke." Do you think their actions justified the treatment they received? Would you advocate a harsher punishment, or perhaps a more lenient one? In your editorial, sum up their crimes, and present your opinions persuasively.

- **Controversial Issue** Huck's struggle with himself about breaking the law is a timeless one. From Thoreau's *Civil Disobedience* to the sit-ins of the 1960s and apartheid demonstrations of this decade, people have been struggling to find an appropriate yet effective way to deal with injustice. In an essay, explore whether you feel it is ever acceptable to break the law—especially if you see the law as immoral. What should be done in such a case? Use examples from the novel and from your own experience to explain your position.

7. Responding to Literature

- **Literary Analysis** "NOTICE," warns Mark Twain before the novel opens. "Persons attempting to find a motive in this narrative will be prosecuted; persons attempting to find a moral in it will be banished; persons attempting to find a plot in it will be shot." Take the risk. Identify one theme that you see in *Huckleberry Finn,* and write an essay showing how events or characters in the novel reveal that theme. Quote specific sentences and phrases that communicate Twain's meaning to you most strongly.

Lord of the Flies
by William Golding

1. Personal and Expressive Writing

- **Reflective Essay** The signal fire is a matter of life and death, yet Ralph can't get that across to the others. Write an essay about a time when you struggled to explain something or communicate an idea. You may have been trying to get through to one person or to many. Use specific details to show what happened and how you felt, and include your reflections about what the experience taught you.

2. Informative Exposition: Classification

- **Definition** The littluns say the beast is a snake, or maybe a sea creature. Simon pictures the beast as "a human at once heroic and sick." How do you picture the beast? What do you think the beast is? Do you think it exists in the real world, or only in the world of Golding's novel? In an essay, offer your own definition of the beast. Use examples from real life, as well as from the novel, to explain what the beast is and isn't, and what it can and can't do.

3. Informative Exposition: Analysis

- **Subject Analysis** Imagine that you're Ralph. Five years have gone by since your rescue, and you're trying to understand your experiences on the island. In Ralph's voice, write a subject analysis tracing the changes that took place in you and in the other boys. Focus on one or more of the following ideas. What might you say about the signal fire, the assembly, the hunt, and the beast? How might you explain the "shutter" that started closing down in your mind? What reasons might you find for the general breakdown of civilized behavior?

4. Persuasion

- **Persuasive Essay** Do people in groups behave differently than they do when they act as individuals? In an essay, persuade your readers to agree with your view on this issue. Think about the behavior of the boys in *Lord of the Flies.* Use examples and incidents from the novel and from your own experience to support your position.

5. Responding to Literature

- **Personal Response** Now that you have finished reading *Lord of the Flies,* which images remain most vivid in your mind? Choose one, and write an essay describing it and exploring why it is memorable for you. Relate the image to the messages about people or about life that the novel conveys to you.

- **Literary Analysis** "What's the matter—frightened?" Jack taunts. Consider the idea that people are by nature savage and uncivilized. Write an essay examining your thoughts about this idea and showing how it does or does not apply to the characters and events portrayed in the novel.

- **Analyzing a Character** Characters that are all evil or all good do not seem believable. Instead, writers create characters that are a mix of good and bad, that possess both strengths and weaknesses. In an essay, discuss what you believe are the strengths and weaknesses of Jack, Ralph, Piggy, Simon, and Samneric.

Of Mice and Men
by John Steinbeck

1. Personal and Expressive Writing

- **Personal Letter** Imagine that John Steinbeck is still living, and write him a letter. Tell him how you responded to the novel's portrayals of racial discrimination, age discrimination, and discrimination against people with disabilities. Discuss your thoughts and feelings about such forms of discrimination, and mention how events in the novel relate to events in your own experience. Include any questions you might like to ask about how or why Steinbeck wrote the novel.

2. Informative Exposition: Classification

- **Comparison and Contrast** Steinbeck describes Lenny as George's opposite. What do the two "opposites" have in common? Write an essay comparing and contrasting George and Lenny, mentioning each man's looks, his strengths and weaknesses, his personality traits, and his degree of isolation from others.

- **Extended Metaphor** Are dreams a beacon in the darkness—always before us to lead us on, or are they recurring mirages that disappear just as we get close? What metaphor best expresses the role of dreams as portrayed in the novel? Create a metaphor for dreams, and then write an essay in which you extend and explain your metaphor. Show how the metaphor applies to the dream shared by Lenny, George, Candy, and Crooks.

3. Persuasion

- **Supporting Opinions** Lenny kills Curley's wife in a panic. Who else, or what else, bears part of the responsibility for her death? Explain your opinion, supporting it with careful reasoning and with specific details from the novel.

- **Persuasive Essay** Elaborate on Slim's statement "You had to do it, George, I swear you had to." Write a persuasive essay in which you persuade readers that Slim is right. Use details and incidents from the novel to support your argument.

4. Responding to Literature

- **Point of View** Which of the novel's characters seem most real to you? Choose a character and use that character's point of view to write about the shooting of Candy's dog. Write in your character's voice, using the pronoun "I." Carefully choose details that show what your character perceived and felt during the shooting.

- **Personal Response to Literature** Think about how loneliness and isolation are depicted in the novel. In an essay, examine the types of loneliness portrayed and explain which seemed the most vivid or had the greatest impact on you.

The Red Badge of Courage
by Stephen Crane

1. Personal and Expressive Writing

- **Autobiographical Incident** Henry Fleming learns that courage, like war itself, is not what he had imagined. Describe an experience in which you showed courage. You may have done something considered as courageous by others, or you may have done something that no one knew of except you. Show your readers what happened, and include details that reveal how you felt about yourself as a result of the experience.

- **Monologue** Imagine that the United States is at war. If you do not join the armed forces, you may be drafted. Write a monologue expressing the thoughts and feelings you might have. What might you hope for, and what might you fear? What conflicting feelings might you experience? What course of action might you decide on, and why?

2. Observation and Description

- **Oral History** Interview someone who has served in a war. Find out what experiences your subject had. Ask how your subject felt at the time and how he or she feels about the experiences now, viewing them as memories. Then present your interview as an oral history. Write a brief foreword, introducing your subject and giving dates and basic facts about the war that he or she served in. Think about how your subject's experiences compare with those of Henry Fleming in *The Red Badge of Courage*. Then write an afterword in which you discuss any conclusions about war and human beings you have reached.

3. Informative Exposition: Classification

- **Explaining Concepts and Ideas** As *The Red Badge of Courage* shows, there can be a wide gulf between heroism and courage. In an essay, examine the relationship between the two terms. Begin by thinking about the experiences of Henry Fleming. Which of his actions are acclaimed as heroic? Are they motivated by courage? When does Henry feel courageous? You also might look up *heroism* and *courage* in an unabridged dictionary. Use examples from your own experience, as well as details from the dictionary and the novel, to demonstrate the relationship you see between the two concepts.

4. Informative Exposition: Synthesis

- **Letter of Advice** Imagine that Henry Fleming's cousin Jack, a year younger than he, is about to enlist. Write the letter of advice that Henry might send to his cousin. Since Henry's views and feelings change over the course of the novel, decide at which point he is writing. Refer to details of setting and action from the novel in order to show the time of Henry's letter. Write in Henry's voice, using the first person, and have him share his feelings about his experiences as well as offering advice to Jack.

5. Persuasion

- **Supporting Opinions** In your opinion, which of the characters' actions in *The Red Badge of Courage* was most courageous? In a persuasive essay, describe the character and the action, and give your reasons for considering the action courageous. Support your reasons with details from the novel.

- **Controversial Issue** As in Stephen Crane's time, conflict and strife in today's world lead some young people to risk their lives in order to uphold patriotic ideals. As a result some young people are maimed, inwardly or outwardly; others are killed. Explore your views about such patriotic devotion. Do you think that patriotism exacts too high a human toll? Are some causes worth any sacrifice? In an essay, take a stand on this issue. Use examples from *The Red Badge of Courage* and from more recent international conflicts to help you present your views convincingly.

6. Responding to Literature

- **Critical Analysis** Before the battle begins, Henry struggles with his concerns about how he will perform in combat. On the second day of battle, he hears the praise of his officers. By the end of the novel, how do you feel about Henry and his actions? Has he earned your respect? Why or why not? In an essay of critical analysis, explore the changes in Henry's character and your feelings toward the Henry that has been shaped by these changes.

The Scarlet Letter
by Nathaniel Hawthorne

1. Personal and Expressive Writing

- **Reflective Essay** From her long ordeal, Hester gains strength, insight, and compassion. Write about an incident when you had to deal with a difficult problem or with the consequences of your actions. What happened, and how did you cope with the situation? Do you feel that you emerged stronger, more insightful, or more compassionate? Explore these questions in a reflective essay.

2. Observation and Description

- **Personality Profile** Ten years have passed since Arthur Dimmesdale's death. The first edition of that influential reference book, *Who's Who in Puritan New England,* is about to be published, and its editors have asked you to write a personality profile of Dimmesdale. Using details from *The Scarlet Letter,* create a brief biography, mentioning Dimmesdale's background and his surviving family. Then discuss Dimmesdale's strengths and accomplishments, refer tactfully to his weaknesses, and show how he is remembered in the community.

3. Narrative and Literary Writing

- **Story** What kind of woman do you imagine Pearl, the "demon-child," became? Did she really marry royalty and live happily ever after? Write the story of one or more incidents in Pearl's life after she and Hester left their New England community. In your story, show how Pearl's early childhood experiences affect her as an adult and how she deals with her own strengths and weaknesses. If you wish, you may write in Pearl's voice, using the first-person point of view.

4. Informative Exposition: Synthesis

- **Interpretive Essay** What does the scarlet letter, the *A*, represent? In an interpretive essay, explore and explain the multiple meanings the letter has throughout the novel. Review the incidents and scenes that center on the letter. Think about what it signified to Hester, to Pearl, and to Dimmesdale. Also think about the community's interpretation of the letter. Does the letter's meaning change as the story progresses?

5. Persuasion

- **Letter to the Editor** Hester has finally died. As a community member, you want to express your views about her life and her character. How do you feel about the community's treatment of her? How do you think she should be remembered? What lesson do you think the community could learn from the story of Hester Prynne? Write a letter to the editor of the community newspaper, presenting your opinions on one or more of these points.

- **Supporting Opinions** The time is shortly after Pearl's birth. Imagine that you are a member of the group judging and sentencing Hester for adultery. Hester has confided to you that Dimmesdale is the father of her child. What do you think about her crime? What punishment would you consider just? In a persuasive essay, present your opinions. Skim the novel again for details about the laws of the times and about the circumstances surrounding Hester's crime. Using these details to support your points, explain your reasoning clearly and convincingly.

6. Responding to Literature

- **Literary Analysis** Roger Chillingworth changes greatly, both physically and emotionally, over the course of the novel. In an essay of literary analysis, trace the changes he undergoes. What theme or message do you think Hawthorne conveys through Chillingworth? Refer to quotations or images from the novel that convey this message most strongly to you.

- **Critical Analysis** In *The Scarlet Letter,* Hawthorne explores the concept of evil. Write a critical analysis summing up one idea about evil that you find in the novel. Show how characters, events, and images in the novel communicate that idea to you, and quote lines from the novel that seem especially pertinent. Also, discuss whether you agree or disagree with Hawthorne's idea. Use examples from your reading and from your life to help explain your views.

A Separate Peace
by John Knowles

1. Personal and Expressive Writing

- **Memoir** Gene and Phineas are best friends—and rivals. Write a memoir focusing on a friend with whom you once had a rivalry. Write both as storyteller and as interpreter, showing not only what your friend was like but also what the friendship meant to you.

- **Autobiographical Incident** "I must have been crazy!" When have you said that? Write about a time when you did something that you knew was unsafe. Choose details showing what the risk was, what you did, whom your actions endangered (or might have endangered), and how things turned out.

2. Informative Exposition: Classification

- **Definition** Which of the two characters, Gene or Phineas, would you rather have for a friend? In an essay, explain your definition of friendship and show how Gene or Phineas does or does not possess the qualities of a true friend.

- **Extended Metaphor/Analogy** "My war ended before I ever put on a uniform," says Gene near the end of the novel; "I was on active duty all my time at school. . . ." In an essay, show how school was like a war for Gene. Consider who the enemy seemed to be, who (or what) it really was, how Gene recognized the enemy, how he fought the enemy, and whether he won or lost.

- **Comparison and Contrast** Imagine that Gene and Phineas are students in your school. How would you describe them to others? In an essay, describe the boys using comparison and contrast techniques to make their similarities and differences clear to your readers.

3. Informative Exposition: Analysis

- **Cause and Effect** Phineas thinks Gene's out for a good time—but Gene thinks Phineas is out to get him. In an essay, explain what convinces Gene that Phineas wants to undermine him. As you plan your essay, think about Gene's personality and his inner conflicts, as well as Phineas's actions. Then explain what you see as the causes of Gene's misunderstanding, and show how each cause affects Gene.

4. Persuasion

- **Persuasive Speech** Imagine that you're part of the group, watching as Brinker Hadley holds his mock court in the First Academy Building. What would you like to say to Brinker? How might you get him to listen and go along with you? In an informal, persuasive speech, write what you would tell Brinker.

5. Responding to Literature

- **Interpretive Essay** Why do you think John Knowles calls this novel *A Separate Peace?* In an essay, explain what you think the "separate peace" is. Think about the kind of peace that Phineas represents for Gene in the first parts of the novel, and think about the way Gene feels at the end. Use details from the novel, and from your own experience, to support your ideas.

A Tale of Two Cities
by Charles Dickens

1. Personal and Expressive Writing

- **Reflective Essay** For the characters in *A Tale of Two Cities,* the French Revolution is a force as inescapable as a "great crowd of people with its rush and roar, bearing down upon them." Write an essay about a time when you felt that your life was being influenced by forces outside your control. In your essay, reflect on what the events you recall showed you and how they have affected you.

2. Observation and Description

- **Personality Profile** You're a reporter for *Personalities on Parade,* a popular English magazine of the late 1700s. The Darnay family and friends have just returned to England after their dramatic escape at the end of *A Tale of Two Cities,* and you've been assigned to interview them. Using details from the novel, write a personality profile of Charles Darnay, Dr. Manette, Lucie Manette Darnay, or Miss Pross. Refer to your subject's exploits in France, and show how his or her strengths and weaknesses came into play.

3. Narrative and Literary Writing

- **Story** Madame Defarge is one tough character. Did she ever have a softer side? Write a story showing how Therese Defarge and her husband met and married. Where and how were they living? Were they involved in social and political events, even as young people? Was Therese in love? Was Ernest Defarge in love? Might other feelings also have come into play? Paint details and create dialogue that will reveal setting, action, and character in your story.

4. Informative Exposition: Classification

- **Comparison and Contrast** Compare and contrast the proceedings in a modern American court with those in either the eighteenth-century British court or the revolutionary French court shown in *A Tale of Two Cities.* Assess the quality of the evidence; the roles of the judge, attorneys, jury members, and spectators; and the fairness of the verdict.

5. Informative Exposition: Synthesis

- **Extended Response** Read history texts and other sources to learn about the storming of the Bastille and about the conditions and events that led up to it. Then, in an essay, use what you have learned to explain the motivation and actions of one or more characters or events in *A Tale of Two Cities.* As you write, be sure to credit your sources correctly.

6. Persuasion

- **Editorial** Social commentators condemn what they see as a rising tide of violence in Western society. In an editorial, explore your views about this violence and its possible causes. Use examples from *A Tale of Two Cities,* as well as from your own experience, to show what you mean and to support your points.

- **Critical Review** In assessing Dickens's achievement as a novelist, Henry James wrote, "He has added nothing to our understanding of human character." Write a critical review in which you agree or disagree with James's statement. Use details from *A Tale of Two Cities* as evidence to support your views.

7. Responding to Literature

- **Literary Analysis** In a literary analysis, explain how one of the following motifs unites the separate plot lines in *A Tale of Two Cities:* (a) footsteps, (b) shadows, or (c) doubles (such as the twin Evremonde brothers, Dr. Manette's two personalities, the resemblance between Darnay and Carton, and the two cities of London and Paris).

- **Critical Analysis** In the France of *A Tale of Two Cities,* one evil results in another evil, but the end of the novel suggests that the forces of good will ultimately prevail. Write an essay showing how a character of your choice from the novel illustrates the novel's concluding theme. In your analysis, consider your character's personality and experiences and the changes he or she goes through in the course of the novel.

To Kill a Mockingbird
by Harper Lee

1. Personal and Expressive Writing

- **Autobiographical Incident** On her first day of school, Scout learns a great deal, none of it from Miss Caroline's lesson plan. Write about one of your own earliest memories of school. What do you recall most clearly? What did you learn? How do you think your early experience has affected you over the years?

- **College Application** Imagine that Scout is now in high school and is applying for admission to a university. The application form calls for an essay about a childhood event that helped to form her values. Write the essay that Scout might write, focusing on an incident of your choice from *To Kill a Mockingbird.* Using the first person, show what happened during the incident, how "you" felt about it at the time, and how it influenced "your" values.

2. Observation and Description

- **Oral History** *To Kill a Mockingbird* is set during the 1930's. Interview someone who remembers that decade, and present his or her recollections as an oral history. In an introduction to your oral history, describe the person you have interviewed and briefly explain his or her background. Mention how his or her experiences of the Great Depression and the beginning of World War II resemble, and differ from, those of the characters in the novel.

3. Informative Exposition: Classification

- **Definition** "Courage," says Atticus, is shown "when you know you're licked before you begin but you begin anyway and you see it through no matter what." What's your definition of courage? Think about the people in your life, and the characters in *To Kill a Mockingbird,* whom you consider courageous. Then write an essay defining courage. Show what you mean by including examples drawn from your own experiences as well as incidents in the novel.

- **Using Comparison Contrast** Mockingbirds, according to Miss Maudie, harm no one, and they don't deserve to be hurt by others. In the novel, both Boo Radley and Tom Robinson are compared to mockingbirds. Write an essay analyzing the comparison. Show how each man is like a mockingbird, how both men suffer at the hands of unthinking people, and whether or not the comparison fits both men equally well.

4. Informative Exposition: Analysis

- **Describing a Process** Mrs. Dubose wants to die free. In an essay, trace the process by which she gains her freedom. Reread Chapter 11, and think about Mrs. Dubose's idea of freedom. Decide which of her actions marks her first step toward freeing herself. Describe the role that Jem plays in the process, and explain which details throughout the chapter show that Mrs. Dubose's plan is gradually working.

5. Persuasion

- **Letter to the Editor** Imagine yourself as Jem Finch. Tom Robinson's trial has just ended, and you are writing a letter to the editor of *The Maycomb Tribune.* In your letter, state your opinion of the outcome of the trial. Explain and support your feelings and your reasoning, and try to persuade readers to share your point of view.

6. Responding to Literature

- **Literary Analysis** In *To Kill a Mockingbird,* Harper Lee calls attention to racial discrimination, discrimination against women, and religious discrimination. She also suggests remedies. In an essay, show how Harper Lee depicts one of the injustices named above. Explain one remedy that you think Lee suggests.

- **Critical Analysis** At the end of the novel, Scout stands on Boo Radley's porch and sees herself and Jem as "his children." Write an essay analyzing the relationship between the children and Boo Radley. How does it develop over the course of the novel? In what sense are Scout and Jem "his"? What does he give to them, and what does he receive from them? What do you think Scout learns about the kinds of things people fear?

Wuthering Heights
by Emily Brontë

1. Personal and Expressive Writing

- **Reflective Essay** Catherine and Heathcliff follow their own feelings and their own rules—which are very different than the social customs and rules of the time. Write about a time when you followed your feelings instead of doing what was expected of you. Choose sensory details that show how you felt, what you did, and what happened as a result. Would you do the same thing again? Why, or why not?

2. Narrative and Literary Writing

- **Dramatic Writing** Encore! Rewrite a segment of *Wuthering Heights* as a dramatic scene. Use dialogue from the novel, as well as invented dialogue, that advances the action and reveals the personalities and conflicts of the characters. Include stage and set directions. You may present your drama as a stage play, a screenplay, or a television play.

3. Informative Exposition: Classification

- **Explaining Concepts and Ideas** The house at Wuthering Heights is less than cozy. How are the inhabitants like the house? How are changes in the house reflected in changes in the people? Reread Mr. Lockwood's description of the house at the beginning of the novel. Then decide which characteristics Catherine, Hindley, Heathcliff, Hareton, and the younger Catherine have in common with the house. Consider their looks, their tastes, and their ways of relating with others. In an essay, explain how the house and its inhabitants are similar, and how changes in the house are reflected in changes in the characters. Use details from the novel to illustrate your ideas.

4. Informative Exposition: Analysis

- **Cause and Effect** Mr. Lockwood imagines himself a rough-and-ready loner, a lover of solitude. Then he meets Heathcliff. A few months later, Lockwood heads back to crowded London. What is it about Heathcliff that causes Lockwood to leave? In an essay, use events and examples from the novel as you explain what you think causes Lockwood to give up the solitary life.

5. Persuasion

- **Persuasive Essay** Nelly can't make Catherine Earnshaw listen to reason. Can you? Catherine decides to marry Edgar "because he loves me," because "he will be rich, and I shall like to be the greatest woman of the neighborhood," and because marrying Heathcliff would "degrade" her. She plans to use Edgar's money to help Heathcliff "advance." In a letter to Catherine, show her what you think is wrong with her thinking. Find an approach that she'll pay attention to, and support your points and counterarguments with examples from the novel, as well as from your own experience.

6. Responding to Literature

- **Critical Review** At the time of its publication, *Wuthering Heights* was criticized as overly harsh and gloomy, showing only "depraved, base" characters. Do you agree with these judgments? In an essay, explain your evaluation of the novel. Refer to specific characters and events to make your points.

- **Literary Analysis** Review your reading log or any notes you took while reading *Wuthering Heights*. Choose a statement or event that made a strong impression on you. In an essay, explain how the statement related to one of the following: an important idea or lesson, an understanding of one or more characters, the mood or setting of the story.

- **Exploring a Proverb** Choose one of the following sayings or select another saying with which you are familiar. In an essay, show how the events and characters in the novel prove the saying true or false.

  Love conquers all things. Virgil

  O powerful love that in some respects makes a beast a man, in some other, a man a beast. Shakespeare

  Revenge is sweet. Thomas Southerne

The Crucible
by Arthur Miller

1. Personal and Expressive Writing

- **Autobiographical Incident** Jumping to conclusions isn't healthy exercise, but sometimes it's hard to avoid. Write about an incident in which you, or someone you know, jumped to a conclusion. Show what happened and what the results were. Do you think those involved learned anything from the incident? Show why or why not.

2. Narrative and Literary Writing

- **Dramatic Scene** You have a chance to be the playwright now. In Salem, several years have passed, and Elizabeth Proctor's three sons are teenagers. Write a dramatic scene in which they ask her about the witchcraft trials. What might they already know? What might they wonder about? What feelings might Elizabeth show about John Proctor and his death? What feelings might the boys show? Create dialogue that gives each character a distinct personality.

3. Informative Exposition: Classification

- **Analogy** What's a crucible? Look up the word in a dictionary, and find out what a crucible is used for. Then, in an essay, use analogy to show how the Salem witch hunts, as portrayed in Miller's play, are like a crucible. Compare the effects achieved by using a crucible to the effects of the witch hunts on specific characters in the play.

4. Informative Exposition: Synthesis

- **Extended Response** *The Crucible* was written during the McCarthy era. Learn about Senator Joseph McCarthy and the McCarthy hearings, held during the 1950's. Find out what the accusations were, who was accused, what techniques were used in the investigations and hearings, and how people responded. Then, in an essay, explain parallels you see between the Salem witchcraft trials and the McCarthy hearings. Use details from the play and from your research, and carefully credit your sources.

5. Persuasion

- **Persuasive Essay** Was John Proctor a hero or a fool for giving up his life? In a persuasive essay, develop your thoughts and use evidence from the play as well as your own reasons to persuade your readers to agree.

6. Responding to Literature

- **Personal Response** The people of old Salem are long gone. Are witch hunts gone as well? In an essay, explore your ideas about the forces behind the Salem witch hunts, and explain whether or not you think "witch hunts" or the behavior traits explored in *The Crucible* play any part in today's world. Use details from the play, as well as from your own experience, to show what you mean.

- **Critical Analysis** Arthur Miller includes his own commentary in the text of the drama. What purpose do you think he hopes to achieve by doing this? Do you find his commentary effective, or does it distract you too much from the play? Answer these questions in a critical analysis. Referring to specific passages of commentary in the play, explain what you think Miller was trying to accomplish, and show what effect they have on you.

- **Literary Analysis** Dialogue in *The Crucible* is a treasure trove of logical fallacies. Locate examples of the characters' faulty reasoning in Act I, II, or III. Then write an essay in which you refer to a portion of dialogue, identify the characters who are speaking, and explain how the reasoning is faulty. Use summary to present the gist of the dialogue, but include direct quotations to illustrate some of the fallacies you discover.

Death of a Salesman
by Arthur Miller

1. Personal and Expressive Writing

- **Autobiographical Incident** Biff wants to tell Willy the truth—but it's not easy. Write about a time when it was hard for you to tell, or perhaps to find, the truth. Use sensory details to show your readers what happened, how you felt, and what you think about the incident now, as you look back on it.

- **Journal Writing to Public Writing** Write a series of journal entries about success and failure. Examine your feelings about both terms, ask yourself how you measure success and failure, and describe people you consider successes and failures. Then turn your journal entries into a piece of writing you can share.

2. Informative Exposition: Analysis

- **Cause-and-Effect Analysis** Biff just can't keep a job. Why not? Skim the play for details about Biff's problems at work. Also, notice which activities and traits his parents encouraged when he was in high school, and which ones they discouraged. Then, in a cause-and-effect analysis, show the connections you see between the values Biff learned in his family and the problems he has as an adult.

3. Informative Exposition: Synthesis

- **Explaining Concepts and Ideas** Willy senses a basic truth just beyond his grasp. "What—what's the secret?" he asks Bernard. If you were Bernard, how might you have answered Willy? Write what you might have said to show Willy one key concept that he doesn't understand. What is the concept called? What has it meant in your life, and what differences might it make in Willy's?

4. Persuasion

- **Persuasive Essay** Happy wants to follow in Willy's footsteps, "beat this racket," and "come out number-one man." In a letter to Happy, show him why you think he has, or doesn't have, the right idea. Use examples from your experience, as well as from the play, to make and support your points. Decide which persuasive techniques would be most effective in light of what the play has shown you about Happy's needs and desires.

5. Responding to Literature

- **Personal Response** To which part of *Death of a Salesman* do you respond most strongly? Write an essay showing your responses to the action or dialogue that you find especially moving. Explore the connections between these parts of the play and significant events or ideas in your life.

- **Critical Analysis** Is this play mainly about Willy Loman—or is it about someone else? In an essay, explain which one of the play's characters you see as the main protagonist. Think about each character's conflicts; ask yourself how each character changes and whether or not the character's conflicts are resolved. What theme do you think Arthur Miller develops through the central character you have chosen?

- **Character Analysis** In classical drama, a tragic hero is defined as someone who is dignified or noble, but who makes an error in judgment that causes his or her downfall. Do you consider Willy Loman a tragic hero? If so, explain how he fits the classical definition. If not, explain what his main characteristics are and what causes his downfall.

The Glass Menagerie
by Tennessee Williams

1. Personal and Expressive Writing

- **Memoir** Most people are "common as weeds," Jim tells Laura. But Laura is different. Write a memoir about someone you know, or knew, who is different. The difference may be major or minor, visible or invisible. Choose details that will show your readers how this person differs from others and how knowing him or her has affected you.

2. Narrative and Literary Writing

- **Dramatic Scene** Tom's final speech and his Merchant Marine uniform tell us that he made his escape. What about Laura and Amanda? What do you imagine happening to them over the years? Write a brief dramatic scene from the life of one of these characters ten years after the last scene in the play. Show how your character has, or hasn't, resolved the conflicts that she wrestled with in the play.

3. Informative Exposition: Classification

- **Analogy** Laura and her glass unicorn are alike: both are beautiful, fragile, and different from the rest. Write an analogy showing how someone you know is like his or her favorite possession. For example, you may have a friend whose mind seems as quick and quirky as the computer he or she loves to work with. In your analogy, describe several of your friend's characteristics, and show how they're similar to characteristics of one of his or her favorite possessions. Discuss what the possession means to your friend. Do you think it means the same thing to him or her that the unicorn means to Laura?

4. Informative Exposition: Synthesis

- **Problem and Solution** Jim tells Laura she just needs self-confidence. Amanda suggests that Laura learn shorthand, or else get married. Do you agree with either Jim or Amanda? Or do you see Laura's situation differently? In an essay, sum up what you see as Laura's main problem, using details from the play to illustrate your ideas. Then explain what you think she should do about her problem, and show how and why your suggestions will work.

5. Persuasion

- **Persuasive Essay** That Jim—what a great guy. Or is he? In a persuasive essay, explain what you think of Jim's actions toward Laura. Reread Scenes 6 and 7, and decide when Jim realized that he'd been invited as a prospective suitor for Tom's sister. Then present your opinion of Jim's behavior, supporting your points with details from the play and from your own experience.

6. Responding to Literature

- **Personal Response** "I give you truth," says Tom as narrator, "in the pleasant guise of illusion." In an essay, explain one truth that this play conveys to you. Show how it applies to people you know and things you've experienced. Use examples from the play and from your life to illustrate your statements and responses.

- **Interpretive Essay** Remember Tom's closing words? "Oh, Laura, Laura, I tried to leave you behind me, but I am more faithful than I intended to be." In an interpretive essay, explain what you think he means. How does he try to leave Laura? How does he remain faithful to her?

Julius Caesar
by William Shakespeare

1. Personal and Expressive Writing

- **Reflective Essay** Write about a time when you took action on behalf of something you believed in. Perhaps you did something public, such as attending a rally or volunteering for a cause, or perhaps you did something more personal, such as resisting a bully or speaking out against something all your friends approved of. In your essay, show what happened, how you felt, and how you decided what to do. Were you certain you were doing the right thing? What happened as a result of your actions? What did you learn from the incident?

2. Observation and Description

- **Oral History** When a public figure is assassinated, private citizens may feel grief, fear, or rage. Further violence often follows an assassination. Interview someone who remembers the assassination of Dr. Martin Luther King, Jr., or of President John F. Kennedy. Find out what happened during the assassination and its aftermath. Ask how your subject learned of the assassination, and how he or she felt. Then write your interview as an oral history. In an introduction, point out which events and feelings in your oral history are similar to those in *Julius Caesar.*

3. Narrative and Literary Writing

- **Story** Portia might have saved Caesar's life by sending him a message, if she had chosen to. Imagine that she did. Write the story of what she did, how she did it, and what happened as a result. Choose details that show what motivated her and how she felt. You may keep the play's original setting for your story, or you may update the setting to a more modern time and place.

4. Informative Exposition: Classification

- **Definition** What kind of leader are you most willing to follow? Think about leaders you've known, perhaps in sports, in social groups, or in student government. Then, in an essay, give your definition of a good leader, and show what you feel a good leader should and shouldn't do.

Use examples from *Julius Caesar* and from your own experience to make your meaning clear.

5. Informative Exposition: Synthesis

- **Opinion Poll** Brutus and Cassius felt that tyranny must be opposed at any cost. Do today's young people agree? Poll your classmates to see. Word your questions carefully. Afterwards, write a report about your poll, showing how you devised and administered it and what the results were. Include your own comments, and reflect on the similarities and differences you find between your poll results and the various sentiments voiced in *Julius Caesar.*

6. Persuasion

- **Editorial** Brutus and Cassius fear tyranny and see no legal way to prevent it. Yet, by taking the law into their own hands, they create disaster. Parts of their story have parallels in many current and historical events. In an editorial, explain your opinion of taking the law into one's own hands. Which circumstances, if any, might justify such an action? To support your views, draw examples from the play, from history and current events, and from your own experience.

7. Responding to Literature

- **Exploring a Proverb** Some lines from *Julius Caesar* have become proverbs. Have you heard versions of the following two examples?

  "The fault, dear Brutus, is not in our stars,
  but in ourselves, that we are underlings."
  —Act I, Scene 2
  "Cowards die many times before their deaths;
  The valiant never taste of death but once."
  —Act II, Scene 2

In an essay, critically analyze either of these proverbs. Regarding the first proverb, do you feel that people's efforts determine their position in life, or do their "stars"—factors beyond their control—have a greater effect? Regarding the second proverb, do you feel that death with honor is better than life without honor, or is life precious under any circumstances? Use examples from the play and from your life to explain your point of view.

Macbeth
by William Shakespeare

1. Personal and Expressive Writing

- **Autobiographical Incident** In Act I, Macbeth has a decision to make, and his wife applies some fairly strong pressure to persuade him to do as she wishes. Write about a time when you bowed—or didn't bow—to pressure from someone else. Show what happened, how you felt, how you made your decision, and what the outcome was. Explore what the experience means to you as you look back on it now.

- **Monologue** Banquo is killed, but his son Fleance escapes. His father's last words urge him to seek revenge. Write a monologue for Fleance, reflecting his thoughts immediately after his escape. In your monologue show how old you think Fleance is, how you imagine he feels, what conflicts might be in his mind, and what he decides to do.

2. Observation and Description

- **Observing Situation and Settings** You are a roving reporter for the eleventh-century Scottish newsletter, the *Weird World Weekly*. For your feature column "Kingly Kapers," write an account of the dinner party at the Macbeths'. Be sure to describe where the event took place (you might quote Duncan's statement at the beginning of Act I, Scene 6, for example), who attended, what they were wearing (for example, Macbeth's "borrowed robes" [Act I, Scene 3, lines 112–113]), what the participants' frame of mind seemed to be, and what happened. You may approach your assignment seriously or satirically.

3. Informative Exposition: Synthesis

- **Rebuttal** Just before the battle, Macbeth learns that his wife is dead. His response includes a famous passage describing life as ". . . a tale / Told by an idiot, full of sound and fury, / Signifying nothing." Write an essay rebutting Macbeth's speech and supporting the view that life does have meaning. Reread the speech (Act V, Scene 5, lines 19–28, beginning "Tomorrow and tomorrow and tomorrow . . .") and notice which points Macbeth makes. Answer each with counterpoints based on your own experiences and ideas.

4. Persuasion

- **Persuasive Speech** The witches' prophecies come true—but not in the way Macbeth expects. Imagine that you're with Macbeth and Banquo when they meet the witches. Write a speech convincing Macbeth not to have faith in what the witches say. Choose persuasive techniques that will appeal to Macbeth, and use examples from the play to show him how the witches' words can be deceptive.

- **Persuasive Essay** No one forces Macbeth to kill, and Macbeth blames no one for his actions. On the other hand, the witches and Lady Macbeth don't make it easy for him to be virtuous. By the end of the play, does Macbeth have your sympathy? Explain why or why not in a persuasive essay. Use details from the play to back up your points and to convince your readers of your opinion.

5. Responding to Literature

- **Literary Analysis** In *Macbeth,* Shakespeare explores the nature of evil. Write a literary analysis in which you explain one idea about evil that you think the play conveys. Show how one or more elements of the play (such as setting, characters, plot, or dialogue) help to convey the idea that you are explaining.

- **Interpretive Essay** The three witches are important characters in this play, setting the mood and foretelling the action. Who are they really, though? Are they supernatural beings who actually exist, or are they just visions of Macbeth's disordered mind? Do they merely foresee and report what will happen or do they in some way influence the characters' actions? Write an interpretive essay in which you focus on the role of the witches in this play and reflect on why you think Shakespeare included them.

- **Exploring a Proverb** It has been said, "Conscience and cowardice are really the same things." Do you agree? Do you think Macbeth would have agreed? Lady Macbeth? Explore the meaning of this saying from any or all of these points of view. Be sure to give reasons to support your ideas.

Our Town
by Thornton Wilder

1. Personal and Expressive Writing

- **Autobiographical Incident** ". . . [J]ust look at me one minute as though you really saw me," pleads Emily near the end of the play. Write about a time when you "really saw" a family member or friend. Whom and what did you see? How did you feel? Choose specific details to show your readers what was happening and which new insights you gained.

2. Narrative and Literary Writing

- **Dramatic Writing** Although *Our Town* takes place at the turn of the century in the small town of Grovers Corners, many of the problems, concerns, and dreams of the characters are not unlike those of people today. Young people still want to know if they are attractive, and they still have conflicts with parents over things such as getting chores done. Imagine that you are writing the play *Our Town* today. Choose an incident from the play that focuses on some aspect of growing up and rewrite it to fit current times. Think about how the characters might act or sound now.

3. Informative Exposition: Classification

- **Comparison and Contrast** How are George and Emily like couples you know? How are parents you know different from the Webbs or the Gibbses? Write an essay comparing and contrasting one character from *Our Town* and someone you know. Mention behavior, attitudes, backgrounds, strengths, and weaknesses. End your essay by explaining whether the character from *Our Town* seems realistic or unrealistic to you.

- **Reflective Essay** Have you ever intensely wished for something or looked forward to something? Did it turn out the way you hoped? Emily was eager to relive one day in her life, but the experience was not what she had expected or hoped for. Write about a time when you looked forward to an event or hoped for something that did not turn out as you expected. Tell what, if anything, you learned as a result.

4. Informative Exposition: Synthesis

- **Essay of Advice** Congratulations! You've just been appointed The Voice of the Future. Remember why the Stage Manager plans to put a copy of the play into the new bank's cornerstone? Imagine that you're planning to dig up the cornerstone in 2001—a hundred years after the time of the play, though only a few years from today. Write the stage manager an essay of advice about what else to put in. Present your credentials as a person of the future, explain why the items you suggest would interest you and others, and show how they would help the Stage Manager accomplish his purpose.

5. Persuasion

- **Supporting Opinions** Simon Stimson says people go around "trampling on the feelings" of other people. Mrs. Gibbs modifies this statement by saying, "That ain't the whole truth." What is the whole truth? Are people basically cruel and unfeeling? Are they essentially caring and helpful? In an essay, explain your opinion. Use incidents from the play or from your own experience to support your ideas.

6. Responding to Literature

- **Personal Response to Literature** "*Our Town* is not offered as a picture of life in a New Hampshire village," wrote Thornton Wilder in his preface to the play, "or as a speculation about the conditions of life after death." What do you think the play is offered as? What messages might Wilder be trying to convey? In an essay, explain one message you see in the play, and show which parts of the play communicate that message most clearly to you.

Romeo and Juliet
by William Shakespeare

1. Personal and Expressive Writing

- **Journal Writing to Public Writing** Romeo tells Juliet that love is powerful: "stony limits cannot hold love out." How have you seen the power of love demonstrated? Are some kinds of love more powerful than others? In a series of journal entries, explore your thoughts and feelings about these questions. Then turn your journal writing into a piece of writing that you can share.

2. Observation and Description

- **Character Sketch** Juliet loves Romeo's "dear perfection." His friends, however, sometimes think he's crazy. How would you describe Romeo? Review the play for details about Romeo, and then write a character sketch revealing Romeo's personality as well as his looks.

3. Informative Exposition: Classification

- **Definition** Adults sometimes assume that teenagers don't know what real love is. Write your definition of love. Discuss what love is and what it isn't, using examples from *Romeo and Juliet.* Show what, if anything, you think age has to do with understanding love.

4. Informative Exposition: Synthesis

- **Problem and Solution** Romeo and Juliet are forced into secrecy because of their parents' feud. What if, just before Romeo and Juliet married, Friar Laurence had written to both families, proposing a way to end the feud? Write the letter that the Friar might have written. Make the problem clear by showing both families how their stubbornness is harming their children. Then offer your solution. Explain how your solution can be carried out and how it is for the best.

5. Persuasion

- **Persuasive Speech** Imagine that you are a cousin of Juliet's, and you're visiting her on the night when her parents demand that she marry Count Paris. Reread Act III, Scene 5, noticing what Juliet says and how her mother and father respond. Then write a speech that you could make to convince Lord and Lady Capulet to soften their stance. Without revealing Romeo and Juliet's marriage, how would you show the Capulets what they are doing to their daughter? How would you suggest that they respond to her, and what would you say that would persuade them to follow your suggestions?

6. Responding to Literature

- **Character Analysis** *Romeo and Juliet* is, among other things, evidence of the way love can change people. In an essay, trace some of the changes that you notice in Juliet over the course of the play. How would you describe these changes? Which do you see as positive, and which do you see as negative?

- **Autobiographical Incident** Conflicts between generations seem to be timeless. Romeo and Juliet feel that they aren't doing anything wrong. Yet, in order to be together they must go against everything they have been taught and must defy their parents. Write about a time when you or someone you know went against all advice to take some action. Tell about who was right, how the people involved felt, and what the outcome was.

The Odyssey
by Homer

1. Personal and Expressive Writing

- **Memoir** Write a memoir about an event that focuses on someone you know whom you consider a hero. In your memoir, show the qualities that make the person a hero in your eyes. Remember that both men and women can be heroes, and that small deeds as well as large deeds can be heroic. Comment on how your relationship with the person has affected your life.

- **Family History** In modern English, an odyssey is a voyage of discovery, usually involving uncertainty, danger, or adventure. The voyage may be a physical one, or it may be an emotional journey. Write about an odyssey involving one or more members of your family. Perhaps your ancestors undertook a difficult voyage to reach the United States, or perhaps they endured a long journey across the country to reach your present home. Perhaps a family member has been changed in some way as a result of an emotional experience. In a family history, write about the journey and discuss its effects on your family and on you.

2. Narrative and Literary Writing

- **Narrative Poem** Imagine that a few years after Odysseus' homecoming, Telemachus sets out to retrace his father's journey. In a narrative poem, recount an adventure that Telemachus has. You may write in the third person or you may have Telemachus speak for himself, using the first person. Emphasize the high points of your narrative by using sound devices and figurative language. Try not only to tell a story, but also to convey a theme or mood.

3. Informative Exposition: Classification

- **Explaining Ideas and Concepts** Based on the events portrayed in *The Odyssey,* how do you think the ancient Greeks who read about Odysseus' adventures would define justice? In an essay, define justice as the ancient Greeks would have. Use examples from the poem to demonstrate how justice might be achieved.

4. Informative Exposition: Analysis

- **Myth** Have you ever wondered if there's a god or goddess of homework? Which deity or hero might be responsible for the discovery of hair gel? Write a myth that explains some aspect of modern society or human behavior. Use your myth to explain causes and effects, but be sure it has the elements of a good story. You might center your myth around one or more of the gods and goddesses mentioned in *The Odyssey,* or you might wish to do some research and include other Greek deities.

- **Extended Response** Odysseus braves even the underworld on his extended quest. Many ancient peoples, such as the Egyptians, the Sumerians, the Romans, and the Norse, also believed in some form of an underworld. Learn about the underworld envisioned by the people of one of the ancient cultures named above. Then compare and contrast it with the underworld described by Homer in *The Odyssey*. Show how both underworlds reflect specific religious beliefs.

5. Persuasion

- **Persuasive Essay** Poor fellows, Odysseus and his crew were really picked on by those mean gods—or were they? How much trouble did Odysseus and his men bring upon themselves? Decide whether you think the hero and his men were the pawns of the gods, or if they were largely responsible for what happened to them. In a persuasive essay, use events from the epic to support your position.

6. Responding to Literature

- **Personal Response** Homer's *The Odyssey* has been read and enjoyed for three thousand years. Why does everyone like it so much? In an essay, explore possible reasons for the enduring popularity of the epic. Do you think there is one main reason, or might the epic appeal to various people in various ways? Explain which aspects of the epic were difficult for you and what you enjoyed most about the work. Use specifics from the epic to show what you mean.

- **Literary Analysis** How do Odysseus' adventures change him? What if anything does he learn? In an essay, trace the changes in Odysseus' character. You might wish to discuss first the type of person Odysseus was before his journey, and then contrast that person with Odysseus afterwards. If you prefer, you could discuss each personality characteristic, showing how it related to Odysseus before and then after his journey. Also mention any ways in which Odysseus remained unchanged.